FABULOUS FISH

ALVIN SILVERSTEIN · VIRGINIA SILVERSTEIN · LAURA SILVERSTEIN NUNN

TWENTY-FIRST CENTURY BOOKS
BROOKFIELD, CONNECTICUT

Cover photograph courtesy of © Norbert Wu, www.norbertwu.com
Photographs courtesy of: Animals Animals /Earth Scenes: pp. 6 (© Leonard L. T. Rhodes, 22(© M. Gibbs/O.S.F.); Bruce Coleman, Inc: p. 10 (© Jane Burton); Photo Researchers, Inc.: pp. 14 (© Andrew J. Martinez), 18 (© Tom McHugh), 26 (© A. W. Ambler); Corbis: p. 30 (© Robert Yin); © Jeffrey N. Jeffords/ Divegallery: p. 34 ; Peter Arnold, Inc.: p. 38 (© Klaus Paysan); Visuals Unlimited, Inc.: p. 42 (© Hal Beral)

Library of Congress Cataloging-in-Publication Data

Silverstein, Alvin.
Fabulous fish / by Alvin & Virginia Silverstein & Laura Silverstein Nunn.
p. cm. — (What a pet!)
Summary: Introduces several commonly owned aquarium fish and offers advice on their care, feeding, and breeding.
Includes bibliographical references (p.   ).
ISBN 0-7613-2514-X (lib. bdg.)
1. Aquarium fishes—Juvenile literature. 2. Aquariums—Juvenile literature.   [1. Aquarium fishes. 2. Fishes. 3. Aquariums. 4. Pets.]   I. Silverstein, Virginia B. II. Nunn, Laura Silverstein. III. Title.
IV. Series: Silverstein, Alvin.
SF457.25.S56 2003
639.34—dc21   2002154610

5190 9257
Published by Twenty-First Century Books
A Division of The Millbrook Press, Inc.
2 Old New Milford Road
Brookfield, CT 06804
www.millbrookpress.com

CONTENTS

WHAT A PET! 5

ANGELFISH 6

CATFISH 10

CLOWNFISH 14

GOLDFISH 18

GUPPY 22

KISSING GOURAMI 26

KOI 30

SEA HORSE 34

SIAMESE FIGHTING FISH 38

STARFISH 42

NOT A PET! 46

FOR FURTHER INFORMATION 47

INDEX 48

What Is a Fish?

Scientists believe that the first living things developed in water. Over millions of years, the first tiny single-celled creatures developed into a large variety of different forms. One line of evolution led to fish, animals that have many special adaptations for successful life in the water.

Fish, like other animals, need oxygen to breathe, and there are small amounts of this gas in the water of lakes, rivers, and oceans. Nearly all fish use special organs, called *gills*, to get oxygen from the water. Gills are rows of feathery structureslocated underneath the curved slits on either side of the fish's body just behind the eyes. The fish gulps water through its mouth. The water flows over the gills, and oxygen from it passes into blood vessels that carry the oxygen to the rest of the body. In addition to their gills, some fish have breathing organs similar to the lungs of people and other animals. They use their lungs to breathe air when they come to the surface.

Fish have fins to help them swim through the water and keep their balance. The *dorsal fin*, along the back of the fish, and the *anal fin*, underneath its rear part, help to keep the fish upright. The *pectoral fins*, on each side of the fish at the back of the head, help the fish to turn and steer and provide power for swimming. Another pair, the *pelvic fins*, extend downward from the fish's lower sides, behind the pectoral fins. A single *caudal fin*, or tail fin, swings back and forth to send the fish swishing through the water. This fin also helps in steering. The fish's streamlined shape allows it to slide smoothly through the water with a minimum of effort.

Most fish, but not all, are covered with scales. These scales are bony disks formed in the skin. They overlap one another like shingles on a roof and serve as a kind of armor to help protect the soft body underneath. If the scales are worn or injured, they will grow back.

WHAT A PET!

THIS SERIES WILL GIVE you information about some well-known animals and some unusual ones. It will help you to select a pet suitable for your family and for where you live. It will also tell you about animals that should not be pets. It is important for you to understand that many people who work with animals are strongly opposed to keeping any wild creature as a pet.

People tend to want to keep exotic animals. But they forget that often it is illegal to have them as pets, and taking them from their wild environment may have serious consequences for the natural community. Exotic animals may require a great deal of special care and will never really become good pets. A current fad of owning an exotic animal may quickly pass, and the animals suffer. Their owners may abandon them in an effort to return them to the wild, even though the animals can no longer survive there. Or they may languish in small quarters without proper food and exercise.

Before selecting any animal as a pet, it is a good idea to learn as much as you can about it. This series will help you, and your local veterinarian is a good source of information. You should also find out if the animal is endangered. Phone numbers for each state wildlife agency can be found on the Internet at

www.rzu2u.com/states.htm

Any pet is a big responsibility—*your* responsibility. The most important thing to keep in mind when selecting a pet is the welfare of the animal.

ANGELFISH

FAST FACTS

Scientific name	*Pterophyllum scalare* (common angelfish) in Family Cichlidae (freshwater angelfish); *Centropyge bispinnosus* (coral beauty); *Centropyge loriculus* (flame angelfish) in Family Pomacanthidae (marine angelfish)
Cost	Under $10 (larger fish are more expensive)
Food	Commercial fish flakes, brine shrimp, bloodworms (found in pet stores)
Housing	At least a 20-gallon (75-L) aquarium tank. Put 2 to 3 inches (5 to 8 cm) of gravel or sand on the bottom. Include broadleaf aquatic plants and rocks for hiding. Provide a filtration system and heater.
Training	Fish cannot be trained to do tricks. They may learn when it's feeding time.
Special notes	This tropical fish must live in warm waters, 76° to 80°F (24° to 27°C).

ANGELFISH

WALK INTO ALMOST ANY pet store, and you'll see lots of different kinds of fish. Fish are popular pets, but which ones should you buy? Maybe you like the ones with beautiful bright colors, or how about the funny-looking ones? You can't choose a fish on looks alone, though. Different fish have different needs. Some kinds make good starter pets. Others are more difficult to keep and are better for more experienced fish owners.

Angelfish are among the most popular fish sold in pet stores. They are easy to recognize with their disk-shaped bodies and long, flowing fins, and they make a great addition to a community tank—but they are not the best choice for beginners.

A LOOK AT ANGELFISH

Angelfish can be found in the warm waters of tropical regions. There are more than eighty kinds of marine (saltwater) species, but only a few, closely related freshwater species. Marine angelfish live in shallow waters, usually around coral reefs. Coral reefs provide much of their food, especially algae, which grow on the corals. They also feed on animals and plants that hide out in the reefs. Freshwater angelfish are originally from the Amazon River in South America. Today they are found in the Amazon and Orinoco rivers and in the smaller streams that branch off from them. They live in shallow waters, where there are plenty of places to hide—among water plants or the roots of trees growing at the river's edge.

DID YOU KNOW?
Fish are the only pets that live entirely underwater.

Freshwater angelfish wander through the waters in very small groups of two or three. These fish are no "angels." They are very territorial and will fight other angelfish that get too close. They will also pick on anybody else that is similar in size and appearance.

Territory is especially important when the angelfish are ready to spawn, or breed, around ten months of age. At this time, the angelfish carefully select their mates, and each pair stakes out a territory of its own. Together the pair will drive

What Are Coral Reefs?

Coral reefs are formed by tiny sea animals called coral polyps. Their soft bodies are protected by hard skeletons made of limestone. Most coral polyps live together in colonies. They attach themselves to each other, building new layers on top of the limestone skeletons left by past generations. Light shines through the shallow waters where they live, allowing algae and other plantlike organisms growing on the reefs to produce food by photosynthesis. The algae then become food for many sea animals, such as marine angelfish.

away any other angelfish that try to invade their territory. Soon they start to look for a spawning place. Usually the eggs are laid on a vertical surface, such as the leaves or stems of tall water plants. Before the female lays her eggs, the spawning spot must be cleaned thoroughly. Both fish clean the area, biting or scrubbing the surface with a leaf, rock, or some other object.

Just before spawning, a breeding tube, called the *ovipositor*, develops in both the male and female, but it is much more obvious in the female. When the female is ready to breed, she touches the leaf with her ovipositor, depositing the eggs, which stick to the surface. The male follows, releasing sperm as he passes over the eggs. Some of the sperm join with eggs, fertilizing them to start the lives of new individuals. There may be more than several hundred fertilized eggs when they are done. (The parents eat any eggs that are not fertilized.)

Angelfish are very good parents. They help to keep the eggs clean by swimming around them and moving their pectoral fins, which sweep water over the eggs. The male angelfish is also on guard duty, protecting the eggs from predators. When the young fish (called *fry*) hatch, they stay attached to a rock or leaf at first. A special glue, produced by glands in the tops of their heads, keeps them in place. Their tails swish rapidly back and forth, strengthening their muscles and helping to bring air into the water and sweep away debris. After about a week, they start to practice swimming, learning to move through the water and find food. Their parents continue to take care of them until they are able to get along on their own.

DID YOU KNOW?

All marine angelfish start out their lives as females. Once they mature, some of them become males. They also change their shape as they grow. The fry are long and slim at first; they get their adult shape by about three to four months of age.

ANGELFISH AS PETS

Marine angelfish can vary greatly in size, from the 4-inch (10-cm) dwarf angels to the Korean angels, which can grow to 2 feet (61 cm). Their bodies are often brightly colored with a variety of patterns.

8

Freshwater angelfish are the ones you're most likely to recognize. These fish have a flat, disk-shaped body, which looks somewhat like an arrowhead. (The bodies of marine angelfish are somewhat wider.) Freshwater angelfish are covered with stripes or patterns, but they are usually not as bright and colorful as their marine relatives. They also do not grow quite as large, reaching 5 to 8 inches (13 to 20 cm) in length, and their very long dorsal and anal fins can add 6 inches (15 cm) to their height.

DID YOU KNOW?
Marine angelfish are often kept in commercial aquariums, in offices, restaurants, and other businesses. Freshwater angelfish are the kind that are most often kept in home aquariums.

Marine angelfish should be kept singly or in pairs since they are so territorial. Freshwater angelfish can be kept in schools (groups); they will pair off and become territorial when they are ready to breed. Angelfish need to live in a relatively large tank. They need lots of room to swim, so they won't injure their long dorsal and pectoral fins.

Angelfish are good breeders in captivity. However, they are likely to eat their eggs if they are in a community tank with other fish around to disturb them. (This is rare in the wild.) If you do breed your angelfish, make sure you remove all other fish. Fish breeders usually remove the parents as well, because angelfish are such good parents that they will spend a lot of time caring for their young, rather than spawning again. After they are separated from their eggs, the fish will spawn again within ten days.

INTERNET RESOURCES
fins.actwin.com/fish/species/angelfish.html "Angelfish"

www.gcca.net/fom/Pterophyllum_scalare.htm "*Pterophyllum scalare*: The Angelfish"

www.saltaquarium.about.com/blangelfam.htm "Angelfish Family Profile"

CATFISH

FAST FACTS

Scientific name	*Corydoras pygmaeus*; *Corydoras panda*; *Corydoras aeneus* in Family Callichthyidae (callichthyid armored catfish)
Cost	Under $10 (larger fish are more expensive)
Food	Sinking food tablets, brine shrimp, tubifex, insect larvae, flakes
Housing	At least a 20-gallon (75-L) aquarium tank. Put 2 to 3 inches (5 to 8 cm) of gravel or sand on the bottom. Include broadleaf aquatic plants and rocks for hiding. Provide a filtration system.
Training	Fish cannot be trained to do tricks.
Special notes	Channel catfish found in North America grow too large for most aquarium tanks, and it is illegal to release any fish into the wild. Walking catfish are banned in many states and are not readily found in pet stores.

CATFISH

HOW WOULD YOU LIKE a cat that lives underwater? Actually, it's not really a cat, but a cat-fish. You can see how the catfish got its name—its long whiskers look very much like those of a cat.

Catfish are very hardy and can tolerate various water conditions. They are also fascinating to watch, especially when they turn into little vacuum cleaners and suck up all the leftover food at the bottom of the tank.

THE HISTORY OF FISH

All the fish you see in pet stores are descendants of fish that lived millions of years ago. In fact, fish were the first vertebrates (animals with backbones). Of course, humans are vertebrates, too, and so are dogs, bears, and other mammals. The earliest vertebrates were fish without jaws or teeth. About 500 million years ago, these jawless fish lived on the muddy sea bottoms. They ate by sucking up little pieces of dead animals along the ocean floor.

About 420 million years ago, fish with jaws evolved; they could attack and eat larger animals. They could also move around more easily than jawless fish. By about 405 million years ago, there were so many kinds of fish that this time is often called the "Age of Fishes."

These ancient fish were the ancestors of many of the creatures on Earth today. Some fish that lived in shallow waters developed lungs that allowed them to breathe air. Around 350 million years ago, some lunged fish came out on land and evolved into the first amphibians. The ancient amphibians had heads and tails like fish, but their fins had developed into short legs, and they could stay out of water for long periods of time. They returned to the water to lay their eggs. Eventually, reptiles came into existence, then birds, and finally mammals.

DID YOU KNOW?
Some people think that a catfish's whiskers sting. But that's not true. They are actually used to locate food.

CATFISH IN THE WILD

There are 2,200 species of catfish. They can be found in tropical waters throughout the world, although some live in cooler waters. Some are found in the oceans, but most of them live in freshwater, such as lakes, ponds, and slow-moving streams.

Catfish are probably the most diverse group of fish. Some are enormous, growing to 15 feet (4.5 m) and weighing 660 pounds (300 kg); others are tiny, measuring less than an inch (2.5 cm). There are also catfish with some very unusual features. The upside-down catfish swims upside down, belly up. The electric catfish can give a powerful electric shock, as much as 300 volts. (That is enough to run a hair dryer!) The talking catfish makes a loud, high-pitched croaking sound. You can see right through an Asian glass catfish. In fact, with a magnifying glass, you can even see its heart beating.

Catfish are famous for their catlike whiskers, called *barbels*. Some species have two pairs of barbels, while others have four, located on the snout, chin, and on each corner of the mouth. Barbels are used mainly for touch and taste. Catfish can actually taste their food before they eat it. Their taste buds are located on the outside of the body, mostly on the barbels. As the catfish travels through very cloudy and murky waters it uses its sense of taste to find its way. The barbels move around from side to side, almost like radar antennae, trying to detect food.

DID YOU KNOW?
Unlike most fish, catfish do not have scales. Their bodies may be naked and smooth or covered with long, armored plates.

Some catfish are mid-water swimmers, but most are bottom-dwellers. They are scavengers, searching the bottom floor for bits of food left by other fish. Catfish are not aggressive, but they have defense mechanisms in case of attack. Sharp spines in their dorsal and pectoral fins can give painful wounds. When a catfish is bothered or threatened, it extends its fins, causing the spines to lock so that they stick straight out. In some species, these sharp fin spines contain venom (poison). Their sting can hurt or even kill an attacking predator.

Many catfish come up to the surface to take a breath of fresh air. This provides extra oxygen, which is more limited in the water. The air the catfish gulps in travels from the mouth through the intestines, where it is absorbed into the bloodstream. Sometimes the catfish literally "passes gas," when bubbles leave its body as air passes out of the intestines.

Like most fish, catfish lay eggs. Some just deposit their eggs, fertilize them, and then leave, never seeing their babies again. Others are devoted parents and care for the eggs and the fry.

CATFISH AS PETS

With more than 2,000 different kinds of catfish, which ones can you keep in an aquarium? First of all, it is a good idea to choose a catfish that does not grow very big—no more than a couple of feet (less than a meter) long. Probably the most popular catfish pets are the ones in the genus *Corydoras*. "Corys" are small fish, from 1 to 3 inches (2.5 to 7.6 cm) long. They are freshwater fish covered with armor plates and are native to streams and rivers in South America.

In the wild, catfish travel in large schools, or groups. So you should keep at least four or more catfish in your aquarium. These fish are peaceful creatures and are not likely to pick fights with other fish in a community tank. (Their protective spines keep other fish from picking fights with them.)

Catfish may be scavengers, but they don't eat fish wastes. They will feed only on scraps of food that sink to the bottom of the tank. (It is a good idea to get polished gravel or sand because they can cut themselves on sharp rocks as they dig around for food.) But catfish cannot live on leftovers alone. Just like any other fish, they need a diet complete with important nutrients. Give them food that will reach the bottom, such as sinking pellets. They will not swim up to the surface to search for food.

Catfish are a good addition to a community tank because they help to keep the tank clean. But the water still needs to be changed regularly.

INTERNET RESOURCES

www.aquariacentral.com/fishinfo/fresh/cory.shtml "Tireless Little Workers: *Corydoras* Catfish make great additions to the community aquarium with their unsurpassed scavenging abilities"

www.petplace.com/articles/artShow.asp?artID=1701 "Choosing a Corydoras Catfish"

www.pet-talk.au/pages/fish/pt_info_fish_breed_corydoras.htm "Corydoras Catfish"

www.theconentwell/Fish_Game/Catfish/Catfish_Basics.html "Catfish Basics"

F A S T   F A C T S

Scientific name	*Amphiprion ocellaris* (false percula clownfish); *Amphiprion percula* (percula clownfish); *Amphiprion biaculatus* (maroon clownfish) in Family Pomacentridae
Cost	Under $10
Food	Commercial fish flakes or pellets. Brine shrimp, bloodworms, or tubifex are a nice treat.
Housing	A 10- to 20-gallon (38- to 75-L) aquarium tank. Put 2 to 3 inches (5 to 8 cm) of gravel or sand on the bottom. Sea anemones may be added or the fish may accept a rock as a substitute. Salt mix (found in pet stores) should be added to the water *before* putting the fish in. Follow instructions on the package. Provide a filtration system and heater.
Training	Fish cannot be trained to do tricks.
Special notes	This tropical fish must live in warm waters, with temperatures within the range of 76° to 80°F (24° to 27°C).

CLOWNFISH

CLOWNFISH REALLY LOOK LIKE little clowns. Their brightly colored bodies and striking patterns look much like the paints on the face of a circus clown.

Their showy looks and interesting habits make clownfish a popular choice for marine aquariums. These fish make great pets for beginners. They are very hardy and can tolerate poor water conditions.

UNDERWATER PARTNERS

Clownfish live in the tropical areas of the Pacific and Indian oceans and the Red Sea. They can be found in the shallow waters of coral reefs. These reefs are home to many different kinds of sea animals, including fishes, starfish, mollusks, and sea anemones. The corals provide a community in which these creatures eat, seek shelter, and hide from danger.

Clownfish are not very good swimmers. They are quite clumsy and waddle through the waters rather than gliding smoothly as many fish do. This could make them easy prey for larger fish. Fortunately, clownfish have their own personal bodyguards: sea anemones. These are sea animals that live anchored to the ocean floor. Sea anemones look like flowers with waving, petal-like tentacles, but their pretty tentacles are filled with deadly poison.

When a fish or other sea animal swims by, the sea anemone stings it with thousands of poisonous darts and pulls it into the mouth, located at the center of the "flower." But sea anemones will allow a clownfish to swim among their tentacles without harming it at all. What makes the clownfish so special? Clownfish and anemones form a kind of partnership, known as symbiosis, in which two very different organisms live together peacefully and both benefit from the relationship. When it is in danger, a clownfish darts into the tentacles of its anemone host, where it is safe and protected. The clownfish may feed on scraps from the sea anemone's meal.

DID YOU KNOW?
Clownfish are sometimes called anemonefish because they are usually found hiding out among the tentacles of bottom-dwellers called sea anemones.

There are more than 1,000 species of anemones, but only ten are hosts to clownfish. Young clownfish are drawn to the smell of chemicals that a particular anemone species releases into the water.

What does the sea anemone get in return? Scientists believe that clownfish protect the sea anemone from its number-one enemy, the butterfly fish. The sea anemone's poisonous tentacles do not harm the butterfly fish—in fact, some butterfly fish like to nibble on them! They can cause so much damage that the anemone dies. Clownfish are very territorial and will bite or snap at butterfly fish and chase them away from the sea anemone. Clownfish also bring in extra oxygen by swimming back and forth between the tentacles. They help to clean the sea anemone as well, by feeding on parasites and debris.

Clownfish are not automatically protected from the sea anemone's poisons; they must build up an immunity. The fish swims close to the tentacles, without touching them at first. It then swims around the sea anemone for awhile, touching the tentacles ever so slightly, and soon it can swim safely among the tentacles. Some scientists believe that the sticky mucus that covers a fish's body picks up protective chemicals from the sea anemone as the clownfish sweeps back and forth against its tentacles.

The clownfish can lose its immunity if it stays away from its sea anemone host for more than an hour. Then it has to start all over again. And if the fish swims into the tentacles of a different sea anemone, it will be stung and eaten. (Certain clownfish can live only in certain sea anemones.)

A CLOWN'S LIFE

The clownfish spends most of its life in or near its anemone host, staying no more than just a few feet (about a meter) away. The female even lays her eggs on a firm surface in or near the anemone. If she can't find a good place to lay her eggs, she will drag a piece of shell or smooth rock close to the anemone.

Before spawning, the male and female pair clean off the nesting site. Soon the female lays from several hundred to more than a thousand bright orange or yellow eggs, which stick to the nesting site. When she is done, the female has very little to do with the eggs. She defends the territory and her family from unwelcome guests, while the male cares for the eggs, fanning water over them. After a week, the eggs are plump and silvery and ready to hatch. Soon tiny larvae wriggle out of the eggs and swim up to the surface to feed on phytoplankton (microscopic plants). Few survive, though, as many become food for other sea animals.

For one to three weeks, the larvae eat so much that they triple their size. Now they are ready for metamorphosis, changing from transparent, tail-lashing larvae to tiny versions of their parents. Once the change is complete, they have to look for a sea anemone to call home.

A group of clownfish in an anemone host has a very strict social structure. A typical clown family consists of a mature female, a mature male, and a few juveniles. The female is the head of the household. She is the largest and dominates the rest of the group. She is the one who chases away any intruders. The second-largest clownfish is the breeding male. The juveniles settle for whatever food and space the adults allow them. These juveniles are all males and are unable to breed. They grow very slowly and remain small, about half the size of the female.

A clownfish can "grow up" only when one of the mature family members dies. If the female dies, an amazing thing happens. The adult male changes into a female and takes her place. Then the largest male juvenile matures and becomes the breeding male. This behavior makes clownfish successful breeders, especially in captivity.

CLOWNFISH AS PETS

Clownfish are striking with their bright, colorful bodies. They are small marine (saltwater) fish, usually measuring less than 2 inches (5 cm) in length. The false percula clownfish is commonly found in pet stores. It has a small, bright orange body wrapped with three white bands outlined with black.

Clownfish can adapt nicely to an aquarium, since they have such small territories in the wild. They are usually sold in pairs. (If you get two males, one of them will probably turn into a female.) Clownfish are very territorial and are likely to fight if there are too many of them, especially if there is a sea anemone available. There should be a sea anemone for each pair.

It is not necessary to keep a sea anemone in your aquarium, since clownfish do not face the kinds of dangers in an aquarium that they do in the wild. But it can be really fascinating to watch the interaction between clownfish and their anemone host. Anemones do need more special care than their clown residents, however. For example, anemones need enough light for the algae that live within their tissues and produce food for their hosts. If you want to buy an anemone for your clownfish, find out which kind is right for your clownfish.

INTERNET RESOURCES

biodiversity.uno.edu/ebooks/ch56.html "Interactions Between Fish and Sea Anemones"

petplace.netscape.com/netscape/nsArtShow.asp?artID=1352 "Choosing a Clownfish and a Sea Anemone"

www.szgdocent.org/ff/f-reef8.htm "Coral Reef Creatures: Sea Anemones (*Actiniaria*)

www.wetwebmedia.com/clownfis.htm "The Clownfishes, Damsels of the subfamily *Amphiprionae*

FAST FACTS

Scientific name	*Carassius auratus* (goldfish) in Family Cyprinidae
Cost	Under $10 (larger fish are more expensive)
Food	Commercial fish flakes or pellets; spirulina (algae) and green vegetables. Brine shrimp, bloodworms, or tubifex are a nice treat.
Housing	At least a 20-gallon (75-L) aquarium tank. Put 2 to 3 inches (5 to 8 cm) of gravel or sand in the bottom. Include water plants and hiding places, such as rocks, a castle, or other underwater structures. Must include a filtration system.
Training	They can learn to recognize you and come over to the glass or water surface to see you. They may also learn to eat from your fingers.
Special notes	This cold water fish must live in cool water, from 65° to 68°F (18° to 20°C).

GOLDFISH

GOLDFISH ARE BY FAR the best known of all aquarium fish. When people think about keeping fish, they typically picture goldfish. But not all goldfish are gold-colored. They come in all sorts of colors, shapes, and sizes. And some of them have very unusual features, such as bulging bubble-eyes and long, trailing fins.

Goldfish are usually inexpensive and are often sold as starter pets. Too often these fish don't live long, sometimes dying after just a few days. While goldfish may be able to handle poor water conditions for some time, it is not a healthy environment. Goldfish are messy, and it is very important to provide them with a good filtration system to keep the water clean. With the proper care, goldfish can live for many years.

THE FIRST PET FISH

Many historians believe that goldfish were first raised as pets in China as early as A.D. 800. The pet goldfish is the descendant of a wild carp, a plain-colored fish found in slow-moving waters in China. Through selective breeding, the Chinese were able to produce fish with a variety of colors and body shapes.

During the Sung Dynasty (around 960–1279) people kept goldfish in pottery bowls and ornamental ponds. At the time, these colorful fish were very rare and greatly prized. In fact, owning goldfish was a symbol of wealth and high standing in society. By the 1500s, goldfish were brought to Japan, where breeders developed some of the unusual varieties we see today. By the late 1600s, goldfish made it to Europe, and they finally reached America in the 1800s.

It wasn't easy keeping freshwater fish alive during the long sea voyages to other countries. These trips would last for many weeks, and there was no filtration system to keep the water clean. As a result, many fish died. Those that did survive were worth a lot of money. These days, domesticated fish are shipped on airplanes, which take only a few hours for the trip, rather than weeks.

Pet fish gained popularity after the world's first aquarium opened in the London Zoo in 1853. At the time, people thought that it was not possible to keep marine fish alive for more than a few days. But naturalist Philip Henry Gosse figured out how to keep fish healthy for a much longer time. Gosse built tanks, where he kept marine fish and other sea animals. He used syringes to circulate oxygen through the tank and replaced the water frequently with saltwater from the ocean. He also controlled the amount of light shining into the tank by opening and closing blinds. The aquarium was a big success, and soon freshwater fish were added to the exhibits. The long-tailed goldfish shown by breeder Paule Matte in 1880 were a big hit.

People were excited about the idea of keeping fish in aquariums and bought lots of fish and other water life. Unfortunately, most of these creatures did not survive because people were not aware of the importance of feeding habits and keeping the water clean. Even the London Zoo had to close its aquarium in the 1870s because it was unable to maintain proper water conditions for the aquatic life. However, the zoo set up a research program dedicated to studying life in the water, including their biology, behavior, and needs.

By the late 1800s, many countries set up fish farms, developing new varieties and improving on old ones. By the early 1900s, goldfish had become a popular household pet throughout the world.

POPULAR GOLDFISH VARIETIES

There are about a hundred varieties of goldfish, but only twenty or so are sold in pet stores. These fish can vary greatly in color, fin size, and body shape, and yet they all belong to the same species.

The many kinds of goldfish are often put in two main categories: single-tailed and double-tailed. Single-tailed goldfish usually have slender bodies and a short, single tail fin; they are fast swimmers. Double-tailed goldfish generally have rounder bodies and a double tail fin, joined at the top; they tend to be fairly slow swimmers.

The common goldfish and the comet are examples of single-tailed goldfish. The common goldfish is the hardiest of all goldfish. It is usually bright orange, but it may also be yellow, silver, or brown. It has a slender body with short fins. If given enough room, the common goldfish can grow as long as 8 to 12 inches (20 to 30 cm).

The comet goldfish looks similar to the common goldfish, but its body is longer and thinner, and the fins are much longer with a pronounced fork in the tail. Its sleek body allows it to move through the waters with bursts of speed.

Some of the most striking and unusual varieties are classified as fancy goldfish. Fancy goldfish have double tail fins, which can be short or long with varying shapes. Breeders took advantage of natural variations to produce unusual color patterns and changes in body or head shape, fins, and tail. Fancy goldfish include popular varieties such as the fantail, veiltail, globe-eye, celestial-eye, bubble-eye, black moor, lionhead or ranchu, and oranda.

The fantail has an egg-shaped body with a double tail fin. The veiltail looks somewhat like the fantail; its double tail fin is long and flowing. The globe-eye, celestial-eye, and bubble-eye varieties have big, bulging eyes. They are also commonly known as telescope-eye goldfish. The black moor is a jet-black goldfish with telescopic eyes. Lionheads and orandas have odd-looking growths covering their heads like a cap.

> **DID YOU KNOW?**
> Some fancy goldfish varieties have such extreme body modifications that they have difficulty swimming or are more likely to develop diseases or other ailments.

GOLDFISH AS PETS

In cartoons, goldfish are typically shown swimming in a small, round goldfish bowl. Actually, that's not a healthy environment for a goldfish. Goldfish are very messy. They eat a lot and produce a lot of wastes, much more than other kinds of fish. Therefore, they need to live in an aquarium with a filtration system. Fish wastes contain chemicals that are toxic to fish and will kill them if the water is not filtered and cleaned regularly.

Goldfish have big appetites. They will be happy to gobble up whatever you give them. They always seem to look hungry, but don't let them fool you into overfeeding them. Too much food can make them very sick or even kill them. Goldfish need to be fed only once or twice a day for just one minute. Remember, the more they eat, the more wastes they produce.

Goldfish are cold-water animals and need cool temperatures, ranging between 65° and 68°F (18° and 20°C), but no higher than 72°F (22°C). They should be kept separately from tropical fish.

Goldfish are very friendly creatures and will learn to recognize you if you spend a lot of time with them. When they see you, they will rush close to the surface begging for food. In fact, they may even take food from your fingers! (Remember not to overfeed them.)

Goldfish can grow to 12 inches (30 cm) in length, so it is best to keep them in at least a 20-gallon (75-L) tank or larger. If cared for properly, goldfish can live to fifteen years or more. When they grow large, many people transfer them to an outdoor pond. They will stay tame if they are fed regularly by hand.

INTERNET RESOURCES

honors.montana.edu/~weif/firsttank/goldfish.shtml "Goldfish Care Basics"

www.geocites.com/Athens/Delphi/8175/gdtype.html "The Droops Net: Goldfish Types. Prepare for Some Eye Candy!"

www.vin.com/PetCare/Articles/KidsAndPets/PCF02819.htm "The Goldfish"

www.worldoffish.com/aquanotes_html/an_gold.html "Goldfish Bowl"

G U P P Y

F A S T   F A C T S

Scientific name	*Poecilia reticulata* (guppy) in Family Poeciliidae
Cost	Under $10
Food	Commercial fish flakes or pellets. Brine shrimp, bloodworms, or tubi are a nice treat.
Housing	A 10-gallon (38-l) aquarium tank. Put 2 to 3 inches (5 to 8 cm) of gr el or sand in the bottom. Include water plants and hiding places, su as rocks, a castle, or other underwater structures. Must include a fi tration system.
Training	They cannot learn to do tricks, but they may learn when it's feeding time.
Special notes	These fish prefer a lot of light. Therefore, you need to provide artific light for the aquarium.

GUPPY

IF YOU WANT A COLORFUL aquarium, make sure to include some guppies. These tropical fish look like they are covered with all the colors of the rainbow. They streak through the water, propelled by a spectacular tail fin that is spread out like a fan.

Guppies are among the most popular aquarium fish. They are very hardy and easy to raise with proper care. They are also very easy to breed, which makes them readily available.

A BRIEF HISTORY

Guppies have been raised in captivity since the mid-1800s, a rather short history compared to the goldfish. In 1866, an English naturalist, Robert John Lechmere Guppy, collected guppies in Trinidad and brought them back to England. These specimens were named after Guppy in honor of his "dis-

covery." It was later realized, however, that Guppy's fish had already been identified by a Spaniard, De Filippi, in 1863, and even earlier by a German, Wilhelm Peters, in 1859. But by that time, the name guppy had already become established.

By the 1920s guppies started to become popular as pets, but their popularity was limited. In the 1950s they got a big boost when breeders concentrated their efforts on developing new colors and fin shapes. Over the next few decades, breeders carefully selected the matings of these colorful little fish and produced a wide range of colors, patterns, and fin types. To this day, guppies are a favorite among aquarium enthusiasts.

A GUPPY'S LIFE

The guppy is a tropical fish, native to the freshwater streams of northeastern South America. Guppies may be found from Brazil to Venezuela, as well as the Caribbean islands, such as Trinidad and Barbados. Guppies will snatch live food, such as water insects and their larvae, floating on the water surface. They may also eat worms, algae, and even the eggs of other fish.

Guppies have an amazing ability to adapt to a wide variety of conditions. For example, although the guppy is considered a freshwater fish, it can survive in brackish (slightly salty) waters. Guppies can also withstand cooler temperatures, dropping to as low as 55°F (13°C), although they prefer warm water, from 68° to 78°F (20° to 25°C). They can even live in dirty water conditions.

Male guppies are much more colorful than the females. The male's striking appearance attracts the interest of females. When they are ready to breed, the male puts on a display for his potential mate. He spreads out his fins and curves his body to show off his colors. If she likes what she sees, they mate.

When the female becomes pregnant, her belly grows plump. However, she does not use all the sperm she received for this set of offspring. She saves some packets of sperm for later use. She can produce four to eight batches of fry from a single mating. Each batch may contain thirty to fifty young guppies. As the fry grow inside their mother, a dark spot appears near the rear part of the female's belly. Shortly before she is ready to give birth, you may actually see the heads of the developing fry through her skin. They have already hatched from their eggs!

Most fish are egg layers, but guppies are live-bearers. That means that they give birth to fully developed offspring, tiny versions of their parents. When the baby guppies are born, they can swim on their own, but many are eaten by other fish—or even by their own parents! In fact, the mother may try to catch and eat the young guppies as soon as they are born. But the fry have a good chance of escaping if there are nearby water plants in which they can hide. The young guppies start to develop their colors around five to nine weeks of age. The males are the most colorful between ten and twenty-six weeks, the age at which they breed most actively.

GUPPIES AS PETS

The guppy is a small fish. The male is only about 1 inch (2.5 cm) long, and the female, which is usually larger, may grow to 2 inches (5 cm) long. Because of their small size, several guppies can be kept in a 10-gallon (38-L) aquarium. Guppies are peaceful creatures and get along well with other species. However, they should not be kept with large fish, which may eat them.

Males are colorful, with varying patterns of yellow, red, orange, green, blue, and purple, as well as black spots or streaks. The females are a dull gray-brown color. The colorful males come in a variety of patterns, including mosaic (irregular blotches of color), cobra (snakeskin), and tuxedo (half black and half another color). There are also twelve different types of fins, such as the deltatail (wide triangular), fantail (small triangular), veiltail (wide tail), ribbontail, double swordtail, and lacetail. In some of the fancy varieties, the tail is nearly as long as the guppy's body.

Guppies are social fish and should be kept in groups of three or more. It is better to have more females than males because the males tend to chase the females. If there are too many males, the females will get exhausted. If you do have males and females in your aquarium, they are likely to mate. However, you may never see the young guppies if they are not separated from the adult fish in the tank immediately after they are born. (Remember, the parents may eat them!) So if you want to breed your guppies, keep an eye on the females. If they appear bigger than usual and have a dark spot on their belly, they are pregnant and close to their spawning time.

Do You Want to Be a Guppy Breeder?

Guppies breed so readily that you can actually start your own little guppy-breeding business at home. You may produce some interesting and unusual fish that have never been seen before. Colors, patterns of markings, body shape, and fin shape are inherited traits, determined by complicated chemicals called genes. In general, there are two genes for each particular trait, one inherited from each of the animal's parents. The colorful wild-type guppies have a lot of natural variation, so different forms may appear in their offspring now and then. By breeding any "different" guppies with each other or with wild-type fish, over a series of generations you can produce a strain of guppies that all carry the new trait—for example, blue spots or tiger stripes—and look rather similar to each other.

Guppies are active little swimmers and can put on quite a show. It is fun to watch their colorful bodies streak through the waters. These are great fish for beginners, but they don't have a very long life span. They live for an average of twelve months.

INTERNET RESOURCES

www.burkesbackyard.com.au/facts/1998/roadtests/guppy_11.html "Guppy"

www.justbajan.com/pets/fish/species/guppy "The Guppy"

www.naturezoo.com/pets/aaa.php?i=133 "Guppy: by Ryan Pyeatt"

FAST FACTS

Scientific name	*Helostoma temminck* (kissing gourami) in Family Helostomatidae
Cost	Under $10 (larger fish are more expensive)
Food	Commercial fish flakes. Brine shrimp, bloodworms, or tubifex for treats.
Housing	A 20-gallon (75-L) aquarium tank. Put 2 to 3 inches (5 to 8 cm) of gravel or sand in the bottom. Include plastic plants and hiding places, such as rocks, a castle, or other underwater structures. Should include filtration and aeration systems and a heater.
Training	They cannot learn to do tricks, but they may learn when it's feeding time.
Special notes	These are tropical fish and should be kept in warm water between 72° and 82°F (22° and 28°C).

KISSING GOURAMI

KISSING GOURAMIS, WITH THEIR pale pink bodies, are not the most colorful-looking fish, but they sure are fun to watch! You can catch a pair of these "kisser fish" locking lips, in what looks like a kiss. Actually, these two fish are both males, and their "kiss" is not a sign of affection. They're really fighting! This unusual behavior can add excitement to any tropical aquarium.

TAKE A BREATH!

Kissing gouramis, like most other fish, breathe through their gills. But they also come up to the surface to breathe air, using a special breathing organ called a labyrinth. The labyrinth is a maze of folded tissue located in the head just behind the gills. Kissing gouramis belong to a group of fish, called labyrinth fish, that all share this interesting feature. The labyrinth allows these fish to survive in oxygen-poor water that would kill most other fish. In fact, if a kissing gourami somehow gets out of water, it can stay alive as long as its body is moist.

DID YOU KNOW?
Usually gouramis get along well with other kinds of fish. But a hungry kissing gourami may use its puckered lips to suck at the scales of a large, slow-moving fish.

There are about seventy species of labyrinth fish. Some of the best-known members of this group are the gouramis, the bettas (Siamese fighting fish), the paradise fish, and the perch.

A Fish Out of Water
The labyrinth is so effective that one kind of perch, the climbing perch, actually climbs out of the water and wriggles along the muddy ground during rainstorms to migrate to a new water source. If it doesn't find one in time, it burrows into the mud and hibernates until it rains again.

How does the labyrinth work? When a kissing gourami takes a gulp of air from the water surface, the air is trapped in the labyrinth. Blood passes through the labyrinth, and oxygen is absorbed directly into the bloodstream. Labyrinth fish have become so dependent on the labyrinth that they could drown if they couldn't get to the surface for air. So even in well-aerated waters, a kissing gourami will occasionally come up to the surface for a gulp of air.

THE UNUSUAL GOURAMI

The kissing gourami is a freshwater fish, originally found in the still, muddy lakes and ponds of Southeast Asia, in such countries as Thailand, Malaysia, and Laos. It is commonly used for food in its native lands. The kissing gourami has a flattened, oval-shaped body and can grow to 12 inches (30 cm) long in the wild.

The kissing gourami has some unusual habits that set it apart from other kinds of gouramis. It has thick, protruding lips, which are used for its most famous behavior—kissing. Although it looks sweet and romantic, the "kissing" actually involves two males in a fight for dominance. Like two rams butting heads, the two male gouramis come face-to-face to test their strength. But instead of using horns, the gouramis use their lips. They extend their lips and press them together tightly as their bodies sway back and forth. To the observer, it looks like they are enjoying a sweet kiss. In reality, it is an act of aggression. Eventually, the dominant male overpowers the weaker one, and the loser swims away.

When it comes to breeding, kissing gouramis do not follow the same rules as other gouramis. The gourami family is famous for making bubble nests. Usually the male makes the bubble nest by blowing little soapy bubbles filled with saliva and air. The bubbles float on the surface of the water underneath plants. Then the male wraps his body around the female, squeezing the eggs out of her body. He carries the eggs in his mouth and "spits" them into the nest. Once all the eggs are brought over to the nest, the female's job is done; but the male is on guard duty, protecting the eggs until they are ready to hatch.

The kissing gourami, however, is the only gourami that does not make a bubble nest. The male wraps his body around his mate, forcing the eggs out of her body. At the same time, he sprays his sperm over them. She may lay more than a thousand eggs. The fertilized eggs then float freely to the water surface, which is usually covered with thickly growing water plants. When the eggs hatch, the fry feed on bacteria and other microorganisms living on the plant matter. Unlike most other gourami fathers, kissing gouramis have no interest in protecting their offspring.

The kissing gouramis are the least colorful members of the gourami family. This colorful family includes gouramis that are a shimmering bright blue color, gold gouramis, dwarf gouramis whose males have red stripes on a silver-blue body, and pearl gouramis whose silvery body is dotted with shimmering, rainbowlike spots. Although the kissing gouramis do not have showy colors like these, their interesting behavior makes them very popular pets.

KISSING GOURAMIS AS PETS

You are probably most familiar with the pink-colored kissing gourami, sometimes called the pink kisser, which is commonly kept in aquariums. But there is also another kissing gourami available, the green kisser, which is silvery green with dark stripes on its sides. This greenish color is the natural color of the wild kissing gourami. Although these fish can grow to 12 inches (30 cm) in the wild, they usually do not grow larger than 6 inches (15 cm) when kept in an aquarium.

Not a Kissing Cousin

The giant gourami is the largest member of the gourami family, growing to an average of 20 to 34 inches (51 to 86 cm) in length. Pet shops sometimes mistakenly sell young giant gouramis as a much smaller relative, the chocolate gourami. The unfortunate pet owner usually doesn't find out about the error until the giant gourami has outgrown its tank and eaten all the other fish!

Now that you know that kissing gouramis are actually fighting when they are "kissing," should you keep only one of them? You could keep just one, but of course, watching two gouramis kiss can be fun. Actually, this is a fairly harmless way to handle their disputes. Generally speaking, kissing gouramis are peaceful creatures. They usually get along with other fish species similar in size. But you will probably see a couple of male gouramis occasionally engage in some "kissing." More often, though, you will probably see the kissing gouramis using their puckered lips to scrape algae off rocks or the side of the aquarium.

If you're thinking about dressing up the aquarium with water plants, you should consider using plastic plants. Kissing gouramis will probably eat any edible vegetation in the tank.

INTERNET RESOURCES

badmanstropicalfish.com/profiles/profile60.html "Kissing Gourami Profile, with tropical fish information"

harrys-practice.com.au/flatsite/0721/petcheck.html "Kissing Gourami"

www.animalnetwork.com/fish/profiles/profileview.asp?RecordNo=230 "Freshwater—Kissing Gourami (*Helostoma temminckii*)"

www.liveaquaria.com/product/prod_Display.cfm?siteid=21&pCatId=968 "Kissing Gourami (*Helostoma temminckii*)"

KOI

FAST FACTS

Scientific name	*Cyprinus carpio* (Common carp) in Family Cyprinidae
Cost	$10 to $50 (more for show quality)
Food	Food pellets for koi. They will also eat shrimp, worms, water plants, cereal, rice, and citrus fruits.
Housing	An outdoor garden pond. Must provide a filtration and aeration system. Include water plants, lily pads.
Training	Can be trained to eat from owner's hands.
Special notes	Can survive year-round even in areas where ponds freeze in the winter.

KOI

KOI ARE LARGE, COLORFUL fish. At their adult size they are too big to live in an aquarium, but they can thrive in outdoor ponds. In fact, koi are the most popular fish for ornamental ponds. Some people have called them "living jewels" because their brilliant colors seem to shine like jewels as they glide through the water.

There's something about watching these graceful creatures that gives you a feeling of peace and tranquillity. However, keeping koi involves a lot more responsibility and is more expensive than keeping aquarium fish.

ORIGIN OF THE KOI

Koi are the descendants of the common carp, a dull-colored freshwater fish found in China. This fish was, and still is, an important food source for people in Asia, as well as other parts of the world. Some historians believe that the wild carp was brought to Japan around A.D. 200. But the koi that we know today was not developed until about two hundred years ago.

> **DID YOU KNOW?**
> Koi are sometimes confused with goldfish. But they are not goldfish. The two are distant relatives.

Koi were first bred in Japan during the 1800s in the rice-growing area of Niigata Prefecture. Rice is grown in flooded fields, called paddies. The paddies provided a convenient place to raise carp for food, as well. Most of the farm-raised carp were dull-colored like their wild ancestors, but some of them had a red color and interesting body patterns. Some farmers became interested in these unusual fish. They separated the colorful carp and bred them together. Over many generations, a number of new color variations were developed.

In 1914 some of the most attractive koi varieties were shown at an exhibition in Tokyo. For the first time, people outside of Niigata found out about koi. They were wildly enthusiastic, especially after Crown Prince Hirohito began raising these fish. Soon koi were being bred all over Japan and in other parts of the world, as well. Many new koi varieties were developed.

Soon koi, which once were wild carp used only for food, became a prized possession and a symbol of wealth and prosperity. They were even given to emperors as gifts. Eventually, breeders established major pedigree lines that were worth a lot of money. Today, the best quality koi can cost as much as $15,000 to $20,000! In Japan, some pedigreed koi are even more expensive, selling for hundreds of thousands of dollars each.

These days, koi can be found all over the world, from the Far East to the Far West. As ornamental garden ponds have become increasingly popular, so have the colorful koi.

A KOI'S LIFE

Although koi have been bred in captivity for centuries and are now domesticated, they still have many of the habits of their wild carp ancestors. Wild carp are freshwater fish that live in the shallow parts of lakes and streams. They prefer warm waters but can handle a wide range of temperatures.

Carp are bottom-dwellers and spend a lot of time searching the lake bottom for food. They dig around, stirring up the bottom and making the water muddy. They use the taste and touch sensors on their barbels to locate food, such as plants, worms, and insects. A carp's mouth is perfectly suited for scooping up bits of food from the muddy bottom because it is pointed downward.

Carp live rather calm and peaceful lives. Their size and bottom-feeding habits help to keep them safe from most predators. They are normally not aggressive, except when it's time to breed. The male goes after the female, chasing her and then slamming his body into her swollen abdomen. It looks like they're fighting, but this is just a part of the mating ritual.

As the male bumps against the female's abdomen, the pressure forces out thousands of tiny, sticky eggs. The eggs attach to nearby leaves. Carp like to spawn near vegetation so that their fry can feed on the many microorganisms that live there. The male swims around in circles, releasing sperm to fertilize the eggs. Less than half of the thousands of eggs that the female lays survive. They become easy prey for predators, and many of them are eaten by their mother soon after she lays them. She may even eat some of the fry after they hatch.

KOI AS PETS

Koi can grow quite large, as much as 3 feet (91 cm) long and up to 25 pounds (11 kg). Females are usually larger than the males. When koi are young, they can be kept in an aquarium. But they can reach 20 inches (50 cm) in three to four years. Unless you have an enormous tank, an aquarium is no longer a suitable home for the koi. They should be moved to an outdoor pond, where they will have plenty of room.

Koi come in a wide variety of colors and body patterns, but only thirteen major varieties are recognized for show competitions. (There are also many subvarieties.) The most popular koi varieties are kohaku (white with red markings), sanke (white with black and red markings), and showa (black with white and red markings). There are also varieties with a metallic sheen and some with shiny, mirrorlike gold or silver scales.

> ## Breeding Basics
>
> *Normally a mother and father produce offspring that look similar to at least one of the parents. But that's not the case with koi. A pair of koi can produce offspring with varied colors, body patterns, and sizes—and none of them may look anything like their parents. Koi breeders work for many years to produce marketable new varieties. When two fish with a desirable trait breed, only a small minority of their offspring show the same trait. The breeders use these few fish as breeding stock for the next spawning. After many generations of careful selection, most of the offspring will show the trait. Breeding for a particular combination of traits, such as color patterns, head shape, and fin shape, takes even longer.*

Koi are most active during the summer when the water is warm. They also grow a lot during this time, storing food in their bodies to prepare for the cold winter ahead. Koi can live over the winter. Staying near the bottom of the pond, they won't eat or move around much. If the water temperature goes below 46°F (8°C), the koi will go into hibernation. They can survive under ice in very cold temperatures, as long as the pond is not frozen solid.

You can tame your koi, especially if you feed them food pellets. Food pellets float, so when the koi come to the surface to feed, they will soon learn to recognize you. Eventually, they may even eat out of your hand. This is an enjoyable way to bond with your koi.

If you would like to keep koi, you need to consider the cost of a pond and all the equipment involved in keeping it running. Filtration and aeration systems are very important to provide a healthy environment. Koi can also cost a lot—thousands of dollars for show-quality fish. However, most koi sold as pets run from $10 to $50.

Koi can become longtime friends since they can live from twenty-five to thirty-five years.

INTERNET RESOURCES

nc.essortment.com/japanesekoifis_okv.htm "Caring for your Japanese koi fish"

www.asahikoi.com/koicare.htm "Fact Sheet on Koi"

www.koicarp.demon.co.uk "Planet Koi: Information about koi carp and ponds"

www.texaskoi.com/Articles/frequently_asked_questions_about.htm "Frequently asked questions about Koi & Koi Ponds"

SEA HORSE

FAST FACTS

Scientific name	*Hippocampus zosterae* (dwarf sea horse), *Hippocampus abdominalis* (big-bellied sea horse) in Family Syngnathidae
Cost	$25 to $100
Food	Live food, including marine shrimps, bloodworms
Housing	At least a 20-gallon (75-L) aquarium tank. Put 2 to 3 inches (5 to 8 cm) of gravel or sand in the bottom. Include water plants, rocks, and corals, and add salt mix (sold in pet stores) to the water. Should include filtration and aeration systems.
Training	They cannot be trained to do tricks.
Special notes	Although sea horses can survive in a wide range of temperatures, they do better in warmer temperatures.

SEA HORSE

WHAT ANIMAL HAS A HEAD like a horse, a suit of armor like an armadillo, a snout like an anteater, a pouch like a kangaroo, and a tail like a monkey? That sounds like a collection of spare animal parts, but it's actually a sea horse! And it's not really a horse, either—it's a fish!

Sea horses are certainly unusual fish. But these fascinating creatures have special requirements, and may not live long in captivity. They should be left to the more experienced aquarium owner.

SEA HORSES IN THE WILD

Sea horses are often considered tropical fish, but they can be found in oceans throughout the world. They can withstand water temperatures ranging from 43° to 86°F (6° to 30°C). They live in shallow areas around coral reefs or heavily weeded areas, especially eelgrass beds. Although sea horses are fish, their unusual traits seem like they were "borrowed" from many different kinds of animals.

Sea horses do not have scales. Instead, rings of bony plates form a hard outer covering, like an armadillo's suit of armor. Any animal that eats a sea horse will probably spit it out because it's too crunchy. Although it is too late to save this life, the predator may avoid eating sea horses in the future.

Sea horses breathe through gills just like other fish. But their gills are not found in rows as in other fish, but rather in clumps, like a bunch of grapes.

Sea horses are poor swimmers and do not usually travel far. Females may roam over 15 square feet (1.4 sq m), while males have territories about 6 square feet (0.5 sq m). Sea horses do not seem to defend their territories.

Unlike other fish, which swim belly down, sea horses swim upright. Their small dorsal fin, which usually beats twenty to thirty times per second, drives them through the water. The tiny pectoral fins, one on each side of the head, are used for steering and stability. Sea horses normally move slowly. But they can swim really fast over short distances, as their fins beat up to seventy-five times a second.

The sea horse has a long prehensile (grasping) tail, much like a monkey's. Just as a monkey uses its tail to hold onto tree branches, a sea horse will wrap its strong tail around plants, corals, and other objects so it won't get swept away by waves and strong currents. It often stays anchored while it feeds on brine shrimp and other small crustaceans that pass by. Its eyes are very sharp in detecting moving prey.

When looking for food, the sea horse uses its long, thin snout to get into hard-to-reach places. The sea horse sucks up the tiny crustaceans like a vacuum cleaner, much as an anteater eats ants. It doesn't have any teeth, so it eats the prey whole. Its simple digestive system does not digest food completely, so the sea horse has to eat constantly to get enough nutrients.

The sea horse has some chameleon-like abilities, as well. It can move its eyes independently, just like a chameleon. While one eye is looking for food, the other is on the lookout for predators, such as large fish, crabs, and seabirds. Sea horses can also change color to blend into their surroundings. Most sea horses have drab colors, such as tan, brown, gray, and black. But they can become very colorful, turning red, orange, purple, or green. Predators and prey may ignore them because they look like a weed or a piece of coral.

BABY SEA HORSES

Some fish fathers help out during the breeding process. But the male sea horse doesn't just help—he actually becomes pregnant and gives birth to live young.

Once the female sea horse chooses her mate, they form a strong bond, that lasts throughout the breeding season, possibly even for life. Sea horse couples are devoted to one another and usually do not interact with other sea horses during the breeding season.

They do not live together, however. The male and female live in separate territories that overlap. The female makes daily morning visits to her mate's territory as a part of the courting ritual. When the two meet, they both change to a lighter color—for example, from brown or black to pink or yellow. Then they wrap their tails around an object, and the male circles the female. They may also spiral around the object together as they sweep along the bottom. When they are finished courting for the day, the sea horses change back to their normal color, and the female goes home.

This courting ritual goes on for about three days. When it's time to mate, the male and female come together belly-to-belly, and the female inserts her eggs into a pocketlike pouch on the male's belly. (The big-bellied sea horse can carry as many as 1,500 eggs, although smaller species carry far fewer.) This pouch is somewhat different than a kangaroo's. Kangaroo babies have to crawl up into their mother's pouch after they are born. They stay there for about a year, receiving protection and nourishment. But sea horse babies are actually born inside their father's pouch. When the eggs enter the pouch, the male releases his sperm to fertilize them. Soon each egg becomes attached to the wall of the father's pouch, which is filled with many blood vessels. The blood vessels carry oxygen to the baby sea horses growing inside the eggs and remove their waste materials. They also receive nourishment from fluid inside the pouch.

The mating pair continue their daily meetings throughout the pregnancy, which can take as long as six weeks. When the male finally gives birth, tiny sea horses burst out of his pouch. They can now live on their own. The father is no longer involved with his babies, and within twenty-four hours he is ready to get pregnant again.

Baby sea horses have enormous appetites. In fact, each one can eat up to 3,000 pieces of food in a single day. Many die because they cannot meet their food needs. Others fall victim to predators. Those that do survive to adulthood can live up to four years.

SEA HORSES AS PETS

Sea horses vary greatly in size. One of the smallest is the dwarf sea horse, about 1 inch (2.5 cm) long. The big-bellied sea horse can grow as long as 14 inches (35 cm).

Sea horses are not a good choice for beginners. They need to eat large amounts of food, and most will accept only live food. Adults eat thirty to fifty pieces of food each day. If they don't eat enough, they will die. Sea horses also eat very slowly and should not be kept in a community tank with fast-eating fish. So, unless you're an experienced aquarium owner and have done a lot of research on sea horses, you probably shouldn't try to keep them as pets.

Should We Keep Sea Horses?

Some people say that we shouldn't keep sea horses as pets. They are highly threatened in the wild. Millions are killed every year. In China, sea horses are believed to have healing powers and are used in medicines. Sea horses are also killed so that their dried-up skeletons can be collected and sold in souvenir shops. Many young sea horses in the wild are eaten by predators. To make matters worse, sea horses are difficult to breed in captivity, which makes it hard to replace the dwindling population. If you want to keep them as pets, buy farm-raised sea horses, not wild-caught sea horses.

INTERNET RESOURCES

www.efishtank.com/articles/keeping_dwarf_seahorses.htm "Keeping Dwarf Sea-horses (*Hippocampus zosterae*)"

www.seahorse.mcgill.ca/backgr.htm "Project Seahorse: Information on Seahorses"

www.stemnet.nf.ca/CITE/seahorses.htm "Gander Academy's Seahorses"

SIAMESE FIGHTING FISH

FAST FACTS

Scientific name	*Betta splendens* (Siamese fighting fish) in Family Anabantidae
Cost	Under $10
Food	Commercial fish food, tubifex worms, bloodworms
Housing	At least a 10-gallon (38-L) aquarium tank. Put 2 to 3 inches (5 to 8 cm) of gravel or sand in the bottom. Include water plants, rocks, and corals, and add salt mix (sold in pet stores) to the water. Should include filtration and aeration systems and a heater. Keep temperature within 76° to 81°F (24° to 27°C), or 80° to 85°F (27° to 29°C) for breeding.
Training	May learn to recognize its owner.
Special notes	Males become aggressive by about two months, and should be separated to prevent fighting. If they are kept in small jars or bowls, the water must be changed every day to prevent buildup of poisonous nitrogen wastes.

SIAMESE FIGHTING FISH

THE SIAMESE FIGHTING FISH looks so elegant with its bright, beautiful colors and long, flowing fins. But looks can be deceiving. This fish was named for its aggressive behavior. Males will pick fights with other males of the same species.

Siamese fighting fish, often sold in pet stores as bettas, are among the most popular tropical fish. Their striking good looks add beauty and elegance to any aquarium.

SIAMESE FIGHTING FISH IN THE WILD

The Siamese fighting fish we see in pet stores look very different from their wild ancestors, which were dull-colored with shorter fins. While their looks may have changed over generations of selective breeding, however, the domestic Siamese fighting fish have kept their wild habits.

In the wild, these freshwater fish live in shallow ponds, rice paddies, and slow-moving streams in Thailand, Indonesia, Malaysia, Vietnam, and parts of China. They can survive in muddy, even polluted, waters with low levels of oxygen. Like the gouramis, Siamese fighting fish are labyrinth fish, meaning that they have a special breathing organ, the labyrinth, which allows the fish to breathe air at the surface of the water.

Like most labyrinth fish, Siamese fighting fish are bubble-nest builders. The male prepares for spawning by blowing bubbles using his labyrinth, mixing in some saliva to help them stick together. The tiny bubbles rise to the water surface, usually under some floating plants. Then the male puts on a display for his potential mate. He extends his fins and spreads out his gill covers; his beautiful colors get brighter. If the female is ready, her belly gets plump with eggs, and stripes appear on her body. The male then chases the female to the nesting site.

> ### DID YOU KNOW?
> Wild Siamese fighting fish eat mosquito larvae and help to control diseases spread by mosquito bites. One fish can eat as many as 15,000 larvae each year!

He wraps his body around hers, and she squeezes out her eggs. The male scoops the eggs up in his mouth and carries them to the nest, where he "spits" them into the bubbles. If any eggs fall to the bottom, he chases after them and brings them back to the bubble nest. When the female has finished releasing as many as three hundred eggs, the male chases her away to keep her from eating them. He then guards the eggs, retrieving them when they fall out of the nest and protecting them from intruders.

In a day or two, the eggs hatch and tiny fry emerge. Their father continues to protect them for the next few days, while they feed on their yolk sacs. However, once they can swim independently, they may be eaten—not just by predators, but even by their own father.

Place Your Bettas

Some people believe that Siamese fighting fish are very aggressive because in their natural habitat they live in crowded conditions and have to compete for space, food, and mates. When two male bettas come face-to-face, watch out! They are territorial fish and will fight to the death, if necessary. They put on quite a show with a lot of chasing and biting, usually aiming at the fins, gills, or head.

This kind of action is probably why betta fighting became a popular sport in Siam (now Thailand) in the mid-1800s. The most aggressive fighting fish were chosen to fight. Two fighting fish were put in a small bowl. Without any escape, they would go on the attack. Although the two competitors were not allowed to fight to the death, many later died because of serious injuries. Heavy bets were placed on these fighting matches, and champions were worth a lot of money. Even the King of Siam owned several prizewinning fish fighters. He also collected license fees for each fight match.

Fish fighting is still a sport in Thailand, but it is illegal in the United States.

THE HISTORY OF BETTA KEEPING

Betta raising started out as a local sports hobby in Thailand, which used to be called Siam. That's where the "Siamese" part of their name came from, but the natives call them *pla kat* ("biting fish"). At first the fight fans used wild bettas, caught in rice paddies, ditches, or ponds, but around 1850 people began to raise the fish and breed them to get a reliable supply of fighters. At first breeders selected the hardiest and most aggressive fish, but as interesting variations of color and shape turned up among the breeding stock, they began to breed some for beauty, too.

Siamese fighting fish first became known to the Western world after 1840, when the King of Siam gave several of his prize fighting fish to a foreign visitor. The visitor presented the fish to his friend Theodor Cantor, a doctor in the Bengal region of India. In 1849, Dr. Cantor published an article describing the fish. He noted that the colors and fin lengths varied and that the male fish suddenly changed to much brighter colors when they were starting to fight. The article sparked great interest in Siamese fighting fish, and they gradually spread around the world.

In 1896, German aquarium owners received the first live bettas, and in 1909, Charles Tate Regan, a fish biologist at the British Museum, gave them their official scientific name: *Betta splendens*. According to old legends, the Bettah were a tribe of warriors, so this Latin name actually means "splendid warrior." Bettas reached the United States in 1910, but they did not look very splendid—they had short fins and yellowish-brown bodies with some faint horizontal markings. The first brightly colored bettas with long, flowing fins did not reach America until 1927. Since then, breeders have produced dozens of new varieties.

SIAMESE FIGHTING FISH AS PETS

Siamese fighting fish are small tropical fish, 2 to 3 inches (5 to 8 cm) long. Females are slightly smaller than the males. The males are brightly colored with long, flowing fins. They have been bred in a wide range of colors, including blue, red, green, black, purple, yellow, or a combination of these. Some may even have a shiny metallic color. The females are rather dull-colored compared to the males, and their fins are shorter.

Despite their name, Siamese fighting fish usually don't bother other fish in the aquarium. But other fish may nibble at their tails because bettas are slow swimmers. It is best to keep them separate from other species.

The fighting instincts of male bettas toward their own kind are so strong that they will even fight their own reflection in a mirror. The females are generally not aggressive, but may sometimes bite other females. If you would like to keep Siamese fighting fish to add color and beauty to your aquarium, but you don't want them to fight, keep only one male along with several females. However, pet shops do sell dividers that will separate fighting fish in a single tank.

INTERNET RESOURCES

ak.essortment.com/siamesefighting_rjav.htm "Information on Siamese Fighting Fish"

aquascienceresearch.com/APinfo/Betta.htm "*Betta splendens*, the Siamese fighting fish"

www.plakatthai.com/drsmith.html "Dr. Smith and Plakat Thai"

www.siamsbestbettas.com/care.html "Betta Splendens, Siam's Best Bettas, Siam . . ."

F A S T   F A C T S

Scientific name	*Asterias rubens* (common starfish), *Linckia laevigata* (blue linckia) in Phylum Echinodermata
Cost	Under $12
Food	Clams, oysters, mussels, snails, worms, shrimp, scallops, bits of raw fish
Housing	At least a 20-gallon (75-L) aquarium tank. Put 2 to 3 inches (5 to 8 cm) of gravel or sand in the bottom. Include water plants, rocks, and corals, and add salt mix (sold in pet stores) to the water. Should include filtration and aeration systems.
Training	Starfish cannot be trained. They do everything by instinct.

STARFISH

STARFISH AREN'T REALLY FISH. Long ago, people started calling them starfish because they looked like five-pointed stars and they lived in the water, like fish. Many scientists call them sea stars, but the name "starfish" is still often used.

A living creature that looks like a star has a lot of appeal. But starfish are more than just pretty ornaments in a saltwater aquarium. They have some unusual habits and can be very interesting to watch, but they can be rather tricky to keep.

Is It a Fish or Not?

A biologist would say that a fish is a vertebrate with a head and tail, fins for swimming, and a brain that controls and coordinates its actions. But people used to call anything that lived in the water a "fish," and we still use words like shellfish *(including clams and crabs),* crayfish, *and* starfish. *In fact, some laws and regulations reflect this way of thinking. In New Jersey, for example, "any marine animal or plant, or part thereof, excepting mammals and birds" is legally a fish, and the California Fish and Game Code states that "'fish' means wild fish, mollusks, crustaceans, invertebrates, or amphibians."*

STAR OF THE SEA

Starfish live in oceans all over the world, in both cold and tropical waters. However, they thrive best in warm-water temperatures. They are usually found in shallow parts of the sea in coral reefs or in tidal pools—little rock-filled ponds that form after the tide has gone out. Starfish share their home with many different animals, such as sea urchins, mussels, and crabs. At times, the outgoing tide drains the tidal pool, and these creatures have to live without water until the next tide comes in. Fortunately, starfish can survive on land for hours as long as their bodies stay moist and shaded.

All the "real" fish are vertebrates. They have an internal skeleton that includes a backbone, and they

DID YOU KNOW?

Starfish don't have eyes, but they have a tiny, light-sensitive eyespot at the tip of each arm. When the sun is too bright, a starfish will move to a shady area.

move by using muscles that pull on the bones. Starfish, however, are invertebrates. They do not have a backbone, and although they do have an internal skeleton, it is not made of bones. It is made up of many shell-like plates fitted together like the tiles of a mosaic. Unlike a snail's shell, they don't form a single solid covering. The many joints allow the starfish to twist and turn.

Sticking out from the plates are sharp spikes, or "spines." The starfish and its relatives belong to a group called echinoderms, meaning "spiny skinned." Other members of this group include sea urchins, sea cucumbers, sea lilies, and sand dollars. The spiny coat helps to protect these animals from predators.

Most starfish are star-shaped, usually with five arms. (Some, however, can have six, twenty, or as many as fifty arms!) A starfish has no head and no brain. Its mouth is in the center, on the underside of the body.

Underneath each arm are hundreds of tiny tube feet in rows down the length of the arm. These tube feet are like little suction cups, which cling to a rock, coral, or some other surface.

Starfish move by means of a special system of water-filled tubes. These tubes extend down each arm from a ring-shaped tube in the center. When water is pumped into the many tube feet, they get longer and bend. The sucker tips clamp onto the surface, and then muscles in the tube feet tighten, making them shorter and pulling the starfish forward. The starfish glides along the sea bottom very slowly.

Starfish also use their tube feet to hold onto things that they want to eat, such as clams, oysters, or mussels. A clam's two shells are held together very tightly by a powerful muscle. A starfish glides over a clam and clamps its tube feet onto both shells, then slowly pulls on them. It uses its tube feet in relays, resting one set while others pull, so it can wait until the clam gets tired and opens its shell. The starfish has a bizarre way to take advantage of even a tiny opening. It turns its stomach inside out and pushes it out of its mouth, then slips it in through the opening between the shells of its prey. After digesting the clam's soft body right inside its shells, the starfish pulls its stomach back inside its body.

A Starfish Surprise

Starfish can destroy a whole bed of clams or oysters in a single night. For many years, whenever oystermen caught a starfish, they chopped it up into pieces and threw them back into the sea. They thought this was a good way to get rid of the pest. They didn't know that if a starfish loses an arm, it will grow a new one. In fact, the arm itself may grow into a whole new starfish! So they weren't killing the starfish at all; they were actually making more of them.

During the breeding season, which occurs only once a year, a female starfish releases a cloud of tiny eggs—millions of them—into the water. A nearby male sends out a cloud of sperm. Some of the eggs join with sperm and become fertilized. Soon the fertilized eggs turn into tiny swimming larvae, which don't look at all like starfish. They don't have any arms. They look rather like knobby little kidney beans, with a small mouth and rows of tiny hairlike cilia that wave back and forth and help them to swim through the water. For a while they swim about and feed on microscopic plants and animals.

After a few weeks each little larva settles on the bottom and attaches itself to a rock with a special sucker that grows near its mouth. There it goes through some amazing changes. Its mouth closes up completely, and a new one opens up in a different place. Five little arms appear where there were none. Soon it becomes a five-pointed star, so small that it could sit on the tip of your thumb. It is very hungry and crawls away from the rock in search of tiny clams to eat.

STARFISH AS PETS

Starfish can vary greatly in size, from less than 1 inch (2.5 cm) to more than 3 feet (about 1 m) across. They come in many colors—green, purple, red, yellow, or black. In the wild, some starfish use their colors to blend into their surroundings and hide from their enemies.

Have you ever seen a starfish at the shore or perhaps in a hands-on tank at a public aquarium? When you tried to pick it up, did it feel stiff? Starfish tend to remain frozen or still when they feel threatened, almost like "playing dead." Probably you have never seen a starfish in action. In a home aquarium, you can watch a starfish bend and twist its arms as it moves along the side of the tank. You can also see its powerful sucker tips in action. Don't keep clams, sea cucumbers, shrimps, or snails in the same tank as starfish—unless you want them to be dinner.

While starfish make a great addition to a marine aquarium, they do require special care. They prefer live food, and it can be a challenge to keep up with their needs.

INTERNET RESOURCES

aqwa.com.au/seastars.html "Sea Stars: Echinodermata"

www.bbc.co.uk/nature/wildfacts/factfiles/418.shtml "Common Starfish: Asterias rubens"

www.peteducation.com/category_summary.cfm?cls=16&cat=1908 "Starfish—Sea Stars"

www.umassed.edu/Public/People/Kamaral/thesis/SeaStar.html "Sea stars"

NOT A PET!

A big news story in the summer of 2002 was a fish story. Two years before, a man in Crofton, Maryland, had ordered two live northern snakeheads from an Asian fish market to make soup for his sick sister. The sister had recovered by the time the fish arrived, so he kept the snakeheads in an aquarium, where they grew quickly. Soon they were getting too big for the tank, so their owner dumped them into a pond behind a nearby shopping center.

The Asian fish thrived in their new home, gobbling fish and frogs, hiding among the water plants, gulping air at the surface, and producing baby snakeheads. No one realized they were there until May 2002, when a local fisherman caught one. He took a photo of the long, slim fish with a narrow, snakelike head and a lot of big teeth, and then let it go. Later he showed the photo to state biologists, asking what kind of fish it was. They were horrified. If snakeheads got loose into the Maryland waterways, they could turn into major pests, eating valuable food and sport fish and reproducing wildly. (A female can lay 100,000 eggs in a year.)

Soon more snakeheads were caught in the pond, both adults and young. Experts debated how to get rid of them. If they used dynamite or drained the pond, some snakeheads might survive. Snakeheads can dig themselves into the bottom mud and go into an inactive state, or leave the water and "walk" across the ground to another pond or stream. Pumping out the pond water would transfer hundreds of baby snakeheads to a nearby river. Finally it was decided to poison the water with pesticides. Secretary of the Interior Gale Norton, calling the snakeheads "like something from a bad horror movie," announced a proposal to ban imports of these fish and their transport across state lines, with penalties of up to six months in prison and a $5,000 fine.

This was not the first time nonnative fish posed a threat to the native water life. Walking catfish, imported to Florida from Southeast Asia in the 1960s, escaped from ponds in a fish farm; within ten years they had spread to twenty South Florida counties and now make up 90 percent of the fish population in some natural ponds. More than two dozen other species of fish from Asia, Africa, and Central America have also become established in Florida, although so far these do not include piranhas. It is legal to keep those bloodthirsty little fish as pets in some northern states (where they could not survive the winters if they were released), and piranha fans claim they are not really as dangerous as most people think, but they could wipe out native fish populations if they ever get loose in southern States.

Keeping fish can be fascinating and enjoyable, but it is also a big responsibility. If you get tired of them, or they seem too much to handle, you should never release them into a nearby pond or stream. They might not survive there—or they might survive all too well and become pests. If you would enjoy watching fish but don't want the responsibility of caring for them, download some "virtual fish" for your computer at Web sites such as **www.virtualfishtank.com**, sponsored by the Boston Museum of Science.

FOR FURTHER INFORMATION

Note: Before attempting to keep a kind of pet that is new to you, it is a good idea to read one or more pet manuals about that species or breed. Check your local library, pet shop, or bookstore. Search for information on the species or breed on the Internet.

BOOKS

Baensch, Hans A., and Rudiger Riehl. *Aquarium Atlas*, Vols. 1, 2, and 3, 6th edition. Charlotte, VT: Microcosm Limited, 1997.

Bailey, Mary, and Gina Sandford. *Choosing Fish for Your Aquarium: A Complete Guide to Tropical Freshwater, Brackish and Marine Fishes*. New York: Anness Publishing, 2000.

Blasiola, George. *The Saltwater Aquarium Handbook*. Hauppauge, NY: Barron's Educational Series, 2000.

Dawes, John. *Complete Encyclopedia of the Freshwater Aquarium*. Buffalo, NY: Firefly Books, 2001.

Mills, Dick. *101 Essential Tips: Aquarium Fish*. New York: DK Publishing, 1996.

Sandford, Gina. *Aquarium Owner's Guide: The Complete Illustrated Guide to the Home Aquarium*. New York: DK Publishing, 1999.

INTERNET RESOURCES

fins.actwin.com/ "FINS: The Fish Information Service"

www.actwin.com/WWWVL-Fish.html "The World-Wide Web Virtual Library: Fish"

www.animalnetwork.com/fish/ "Aquarium Frontiers"

www.aquariacentral.com/ "Aquaria Central—Freshwater and Marine Aquarium Fish"

www.fish2u.com/ "Tropical Aquarium Fish Shipped Directly to Your Door!—Fish2U.Com"

www.fishlinkcentral.com/ "Fish Link Central: Your Guide to Aquarium Resources on the Internet"

INDEX

Page numbers in *italics* refer to illustrations.

algae, 7, 17, 23
amphibians, ancient, 11
angelfish, *6*, 7–9

barbels, 12
betta (*see* Siamese fighting fish)
birds, 11
black moor goldfish, 20, 21
bubble-eye goldfish, 20, 21, 39–40
butterfly fish, 16–17

Cantor, Theodor, 41
carp, 31, 32
catfish, *10*, 11–13
celestial-eye goldfish, 20, 21
chocolate gourami, 29
clownfish, *14*, 15–17
comet goldfish, 20
common goldfish, 20
Corydoras, 13

De Filippi, 23
double-tailed goldfish, 20

echinoderms, 44

fantail goldfish, 20, 21
filtration systems, 19, 21, 33
fish fighting, 40
fry, 8, 24

giant gourami, 29
globe-eye goldfish, 20, 21
goldfish, *18*, 19–21, 31
Gosse, Philip Henry, 20
gourami, *26*, 27–29
guppy, *22*, 23–25
Guppy, Robert John Lechmere, 23

hibernation, 33

invertebrates, 44

kissing gourami, *26*, 27–29
kohaku koi, 33
koi, *30*, 31–33

labryrinth fish, 27, 39
lionhead (ranchu) goldfish, 20, 21
lunged fishes, 11

mammals, 11
Matte, Paule, 20
metamorphosis, 16

Norton, Gale, 46

oranda goldfish, 20, 21
ovipositor, 8

paddies, 31
paradise fish, 27
perch, 27
Peters, Wilhelm, 23
phytoplankton, 16
piranha, 46

rainbow fish, 23
Regan, Charles Tate, 41
reptiles, 11

sanke koi, 33
sea anemone, 15–17
sea horse, *34*, 35–37
showa koi, 33
Siamese fighting fish, 27, *38*, 39–41
single-tailed goldfish, 20
snakehead, 46
spawning, 7–9, 16
starfish, *42*, 43–45
symbiosis, 15

talking catfish, 12
telescope-eye goldfish, 21
territoriality, 7–9

upside-down catfish, 12

veiltail goldfish, 20, 21
venom, 12
vertebrates, 11

walking catfish, 12, 46